The Adventures of Maddie

Meet Maddie

The Adventures of Maddie: *Meet Maddie*

To my M's,

You are my strength and my inspiration.

You have taught me the meaning of unconditional love.

Everything I am is for you.

My Loves…My Life…My Joy!

-Mommy

The Adventures of Maddie® is a trademark of Evan Grace Publishing

The Adventures of Maddie: Meet Maddie Text copyright © 2013 by Monyetta Shaw

Illustrations copyright © 2013 by David Harrington

Evan Grace Publishing
a division of The Evan Grace Group, LLC
5184 McGinnis Ferry Road
Alpharetta, GA 30005

Visit our website at www.theevangracegroup.com

Evan Grace Publishing's name and logo are trademarks of The Evan Grace Group, LLC.

Printed in the United States of America.

Library of Congress Cataloging-in-Publication Data
Shaw, Monyetta.
The Adventures of Maddie: Meet Maddie by Monyetta Shaw
Cover and Interior Illustration by David Harrington – 1st ed.
p.   cm. – The Adventures of Maddie
Summary: The reader is introduced to Maddie, her interest, friends, and family.
ISBN 978-0-578-11880-2
1. Children 2. Family
2013

The Adventures of Maddie

Meet Maddie

By Monyetta Shaw

Illustrated by
David Harrington

The Evan Grace Group

Let's go! Let's go! There is so much to see.

My name is Maddie, come take an adventure with me.

I am a girl, that is so plain to see.

Let me introduce you to some cool things about me.

I like

to skip,

twirl,

and I love

to play.

Life is so much fun when you run around all day.

Take a tour of my room, there are so many things around;

toys, dolls, and bears, but the best is my princess crown!

When I play with my friends, I like to share.

Grandma says be nice to others and always play fair.

My mommy can dance and my daddy can sing.

"WOW" look! I can do both of those things.

Yes, I play sports and I play to win.

But if not, I still smile, we are all winners in the end.

In school I focus and stay on the right path.

I study hard in all my subjects, but my favorite is math.

At bedtime, I'm not sad because I need my rest.

I hug Mommy and Daddy good night, their hugs are the best!

I could keep going because fun is my middle name.

When you are with Maddie, no day is quite the same.

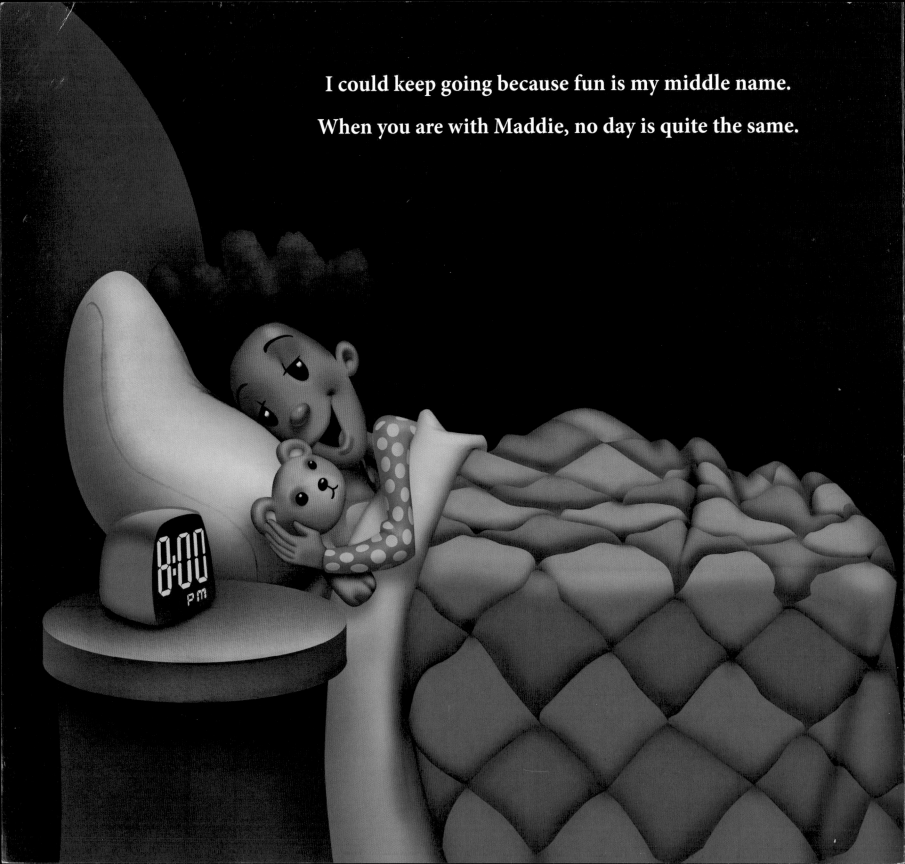

The Adventures of

Maddie

Maddie goes to School